The 360% team leader

How to become a successful and eccentric 21st century team leader

All rights reserved. No part of this publication may be reproduced, distributed, or transmitted in any form or by any means, including photocopying, recording, or other electronic or mechanical methods, without the prior written permission of the publisher, except in the case of brief quotations embodied in critical reviews and certain other noncommercial uses permitted by copyright law.

Copyright © Aaron Mason ,2024.

Table of Contents

[Chapter 1](#)

[Chapter 2](#)

[Chapter 3](#)

[Chapter 4](#)

[Chapter 5](#)

Chapter 1

Introduction

Focusing on effective team leaders is one of the most important aspects of team management for a company, and it is also one of the most important areas. Quality management is the second most important factor in determining whether or not an employee will remain with the company. In order to keep up with the ever-evolving business environment, it is important to continually upgrade your leadership skills, even if you do not feel that your current talents should be improved. In order to develop the skills and capabilities necessary to become an exceptional leader, you have more time than you believe you have.

The Project Management Institute (PMI), a non-profit organization whose mission is to improve the project management profession, is the institution that is responsible for issuing the Online Training Project Management Professional (PMP) certification, which is the most prestigious one in the world. To assist you in gaining a better grasp of how to achieve more consistent results that encourage long-term organizational success, we have compiled a list of several critical guidelines for team leadership. You may learn more about "how to lead a team?" by reading the blog posted on the website."

What is Team Leading?

The activity of encouraging individuals to perform in a specific way is known as team leadership. People are able to realize their full potential when they are stimulated and engaged by effective team leadership, which enables them to reach their full potential. In a nutshell, a team leader oversees, advises, and supports the team while also managing its general functioning.

Although managing a team could seem daunting, it is a skill mastered with experience. The activities that you do as the leader of the team have a significant impact on the organization. A result of this is that you need to adopt some characteristics that will assist you in becoming a more effective leader.

A team leader is in charge of supervising the operation of a group. This function attempts to offer team members advice, support, and guidance to fulfill assigned duties efficiently. Group leader tasks often do not require taking on inherent management responsibilities like employee discipline or annual performance assessments. Instead, the team leader serves as a communicator, problem-solver, resource manager, motivator, and performance monitor to get the task done.

A brilliant team leader may be the difference between a high-performing team, and an unsuccessful one. This book will cover the roles and traits of a good team leader, and provide suggestions on how to become one.

How do you define a team leader?

Imagine a team where the leader encourages each member to accomplish their best job, helps them develop professionally, delivers clarity amid evolving goals, and trusts them to execute their responsibilities.

Now imagine a team where the leader belittles others, micromanages their work, withholds information, and pits people against one other.

Which do you think is more likely to be a high-performing team?

A team leader's ability to encourage, motivate, advise, and coach their teams may impact anything from employee engagement and development to retention and productivity. What's more, research reveals that a team leader has the most immediate and profound impact on the experience of the members on the team. That means having the necessary talents and behaviors in leadership roles may affect how quickly team members develop new skills, whether they feel included and encouraged, and how creative or unique the team's ideas are.

Investing in leadership development may help teams—and organizations—really shine.

Team leader responsibilities

A team leader's day-to-day activities often vary widely by function, but there are many attributes the finest leaders have in common. Great team leaders:

Manage the work

The greatest leaders control their team's work. They plan, organize, assign, distribute resources, and assure the completion of the team's duties. The team looks to the leader for clarity on what to achieve and what matters most. They should be able to look across their team and foresee what will be necessary in order to meet the team's goals. For example, when a deadline changes, the team leader needs to analyze what work may need to be interrupted and whether team members need to reprioritize how they are spending their time.

Coach their people.

The team leader acts as a coach and advisor, helping team members understand how they're performing, giving feedback on how they could be more effective, and sitting side-by-side with them to demonstrate skills like problem-solving, listening, collaboration, or specific hard skills "in the flow of work." They may suggest a certification program for a team member who needs to master a skill or connect them to a colleague across the company who has that expertise. Through their actions every day, team leaders model behaviors and skills for their team members. For example, some companies push personnel to be more open-minded or compassionate. The team leader shows the way.

Communicate information.

Team leaders are meant to engage honestly and effectively with their team. They need to offer updates, share information, and define targets and expectations. In truth, many organizations rely on managers to convey essential news and updates with their personnel as a regular necessity of the role.

Act as change agents.

Organizations are ever-changing, and this may pose a range of difficulties. Because of their impact on the team, it is incumbent on the team leader to function as a change agent: becoming a champion for change and helping colleagues realize how those changes will benefit them. For example, when firms are rebuilt, the group leader could assist the team by talking about how new roles and responsibilities will help them grow.

Inspire their comrades.

The greatest leaders help move their teams forward by helping individuals realize the wider picture of what they're working for, and why. When a team leader talks about how she finds meaning in the job, it helps team members explore their own purpose in the work. An inspirational leader may aid build the team's resilience, boost the team's enthusiasm, drive them to create their finest work, and keep them focused on the future.

Chapter 2

10 traits every great leader demonstrates

While leaders come in many shapes and sizes, there are few fundamental traits that they all share. Great team leaders have:

Functional and technical knowledge.

A primary feature of an effective team leader is that they possess the functional and technical expertise for which the team is responsible. The team leader's capacity to coach and advise their team comes from their own abilities and knowledge in relevant areas.

Emotional intelligence.

Not surprisingly, having functional skill isn't enough; great team leaders must have emotional intelligence to build good working connections. Daniel Goleman views emotional intelligence as the ability to recognize and manage one's own emotions as well as sense and impact others' emotions. In order to accomplish so, one requires self-awareness, self-regulation, motivation, empathy, and social skills. Team leaders who are emotionally smart better manage stress, engage their team members, and enhance their team's performance.

Relationship-building talents.

Team leaders have to develop relationships within their teams, with other team leaders, and across the organization. Ensuring that these relationships are firm enables the team to be successful and helps to develop trust and intimacy.

The ability to provide comments.

Great team leaders must be able to provide feedback on things that team members accomplish well, and in areas in which team members may improve. They lean into these potentially uncomfortable situations because they recognize that offering criticism to the team is a gift that will assist them to be more successful.

A zeal for recognizing others.

Great team leaders don't grab credit for others' work. In fact, they appreciate others' triumphs and make sure team members get the recognition they deserve. The greatest team leaders seek to grasp how each team member wants to be recognized in order to meet the expectations of their team.

Influence.

In order to function most effectively, excellent leaders must be able to influence others. This applies whether they are encouraging their own team to accomplish exceptional work or convincing other teams to engage in new ways. Leaders usually cannot force certain activities but must develop techniques to encourage individuals to comply.

A growth mindset.

People with growth mindsets assume that intelligence, abilities, and talents can be enhanced; they tend to enjoy problems and attempt to continually learn. Team leaders who display a growth mindset inspire their team members to see obstacles and setbacks as opportunities to learn and better. They help their teams feel comfortable taking risks and push them to make the effort to improve.

Self-awareness.

The greatest leaders possess two types of self-awareness: internal and outer. Internal self-awareness encourages individuals to understand their own talents and potential. External self-awareness is their ability to comprehend the effect they have on others and how they are viewed. Self-awareness allows leaders a clearer view of where they needI'm help, how they should rely on the team, and where they should look for advancement.

Curiosity.

Great team leaders are interested and listen to others. Rather than believing they know all of the answers, they ask questions and seek to learn. Without curiosity and the ongoing urge to learn, leaders stop changing and could become stagnant.

Strong ethics and a welcoming mentality.

How one leads matters, and team members look to the example that the team leader sets. For these reasons, it's important that the team leader behave in accordance with a strong set of ethics, honoring the company's values and holding oneself and others to a high level. In addition, group leaders need to discover and accept variety among team members and assure that team members may present their actual selves to work.

6 techniques to become an effective team leader

All leaders have the capacity to develop and become even more successful. Below are 6 strategies to become an effective team leader:

Learn to lead yourself first.

The best leaders lead themselves before they lead others. What does this look like? Make sure you thoroughly comprehend your strengths and possibilities and know how you are regarded by others. Take attempts to examine what motivates you and the type of effect you'd like to create on others. Increasing your self-awareness in these ways may be a lifelong pursuit that helps you lead others most effectively.

Seek feedback: up, down, and across.

Great team leaders not only share feedback with their teams; they also search for and obtain input from diverse sources. They want to understand how they are impacting others. To maximize feedback, leaders should explain where they are aiming to improve and then urge individuals to let them know when they're doing things that damage or help.

Be open to innovative ideas.

Leaders play a crucial role in inspiring their staff to voice their ideas and opinions. Remaining open to new ideas encourages innovation, rather than permitting teams to get locked in old habits of behavior.

Push yourself outside of your comfort zone. When we're too relaxed, we're not learning. When leaders push themselves to take risks, they are creating a positive example for their team and giving them permission to do the same. If you fail, don't be frightened to say so. Share what you've learned from your errors, and that you won't let them stop you from doing new things in the future.

Pay attention to team dynamics.

It could be easy to get caught up in routine chores, but group leaders need to take a step back to check in on team dynamics. Ask yourself: how is the team operating? Where are things running smoothly and where does the team feel most challenged? How are the individuals on my team, and how healthy are the ties among them? Take the effort to build stronger relationships, and handle emerging issues before they bloom into serious ones.

Measure the performance of your team in several areas.

High-performing teams produce exceptional results, and they do it by tuning into their process and relationships. It isn't enough to measure what the team accomplishes. Team leaders also need to analyze how the task gets done and what the relationships are like on the team. Team leaders that expect outstanding results at the sacrifice of process and relationships make it challenging for their teams to continue to be productive together over time. Paying attention to results, process, and relationships holistically helps to secure the team's long-term success.

Chapter 3

Now that you are familiar with team-leading, let us assess their relevance.

What are the Benefits of Having a Team Leader?

Because some operations are too large for a single manager to handle, corporations add a second layer of management in the form of a team leader. Although the manager's function is relocated down a rung, they retain responsibility.

The roles of team leaders and managers are distinct. For example, unlike managers, team leaders will not command, revise plans, enforce rules, or develop their teams by hiring and dismissing. But, team leaders within a corporation generally perform a motivational and inspirational duty. In addition, they're outstanding mediators and link builders, bridging the gap between labor and management. Finally, they may move projects forward when they apply their leadership abilities.

After studying the benefits of team leadership, let us now analyze some of their duties.

What are the Responsibilities of a Team Leader?

A team leader's role is to define targets, evaluate progress, encourage and give guidance and aid to achieve duties. Employee punishment and annual performance assessments are not commonly entrusted to team leaders. They do, however, operate as a communicator, problem-solver, and resource for teams to attain specified objectives. A team leader's major duties are as follows:

Choose team members who have the skill sets essential to complete a specified task

Develop and implement strategies for team members to reach the aim

Assign assignments to team members based on their strengths and skill sets

Provide the training required to perform defined tasks to reach the purpose

Encourage and encourage team members continually to keep them interested and working for a same aim

Oversee a team's day-to-day activities

To assure that the project is done on time, keep track of each team member's work and engagement

Create and disseminate project progress reports to management regularly

Ascertain that resources are being used effectively

Duties Of a Team Leader in the Workplace

Team leaders are crucial in various working circumstances because they are in charge of delegating, supervising, and leading team members to ensure that duties and projects are performed. While team members aren't normally in management jobs, they lead teams of workers and carry out the tasks that come with that degree of responsibility.

Now that you have mastered the roles and responsibilities of a team leader, we will study how a team leader leads the team for the first time.

How to Lead the Team for the Very First Time?

Leading a team for the first time, whether you're building one from zero or taking over an established one, may be terrifying. There is no basis to build on in terms of personal experience. If you're a first-time team leader, you're probably either looking forward to the task or pondering quitting—or a combination of the two. Furthermore, more teams are working remotely or adopting a mix strategy of in-office and homework.

As a result, today's young leaders have a lot more on their plates than ever before. Here are a few tips for those aspiring team leaders:

1. Get To Know Your Team

Leadership is all about influencing your team to reach its goals. If you don't get to know your team members and what makes them tick, you'll have a hard time with this. While it may be tempting to rush right in and make important steps straight away, bear in mind that you're not there to flaunt your ego.

Take the time to listen to your team members, learn about their concerns and goals, collect recommendations, and discover prospective strengths and constraints. Only then can you design a leadership strategy that has a likelihood of success. The first step in connecting with the team and winning their respect and trust is to get to know who you'll be working with. The ancient phrase "listen twice as much" applies here.

Make contact with your team, particularly those who may be having issues. Once or twice a week, new team leaders successfully hold fast 10-15 minute check-in conversations. You may even offer "office hours" on your calendar where people may plan appointments and connect with you if they need assistance or want to speak.

2. Clearly Communicate

Communication is one of the most crucial components of managing a team efficiently. Successful leaders communicate their expectations to their people in a way that is both clear and persuasive. Communication, on the other hand, should be a two-way street. You should retain your doors open in addition to gaining the talent of persuading. Actively listen to your team members' thoughts and perspectives and react properly.

3. Make Time For Leadership

Team leaders must commit time to the role to be effective. But tragically, this task is generally only added to someone's already massive to-do list, putting the new leader up for failure.

You must be visible to the team and ready to help them as a team leader. Fostering a positive working environment and community is crucial for your new leadership post. You won't be as visible or able to aid your team if you're preoccupied with your critical hands-on activities. So, before taking on a leadership job, make sure you review and re-negotiate your workload.

4. Get Your Employees Involved

Employee involvement may be a significant drive for a firm. Working with and managing your colleagues as a team leader puts you on the front lines. Your team members will feel valued at work if you offer timely feedback and emphasize their best interests. They'll take ownership of you and your work. Your employee engagement features may empower your people and keep them focused on their aims.

5. Be Honest and Kind

When your coworkers make blunders, managing a team may be tough. Make it plain to your personnel that it's always preferable to fail and learn from their failures. You are a mentor as well as a leader. You may help your people in learning from their missteps. On the flip hand, some workers may be overachievers who excel at their job. This should not preclude you from giving each team member equal weight.

After learning how to lead a team for the first time, we will analyze how to lead a team effectively.

How to Lead a Team Effectively?

Professionals considering taking on the post of manager must have strong leadership qualities. While managing a team may appear to be a pleasant and straightforward task, it comes with a wide list of obligations. As a manager, you must demonstrate great team management abilities and guarantee that your team members get the most out of their employment. The job is both intriguing and demanding. So, here are a few techniques that aid you lead your crew properly.

1. Set Goals? & Track Progress

Make a list of your objectives and keep track of your progress toward accomplishing them. Set individual and collective targets for your team, and keep track of how close you are to attaining them. This may seem self-evident at first, but we get caught up in daily client requests and monthly reports all too frequently, and the bigger purpose or vision slips away.

Setting and achieving milestones may offer you a clear sense of the team's overall efficiency and daily growth, even if your targets aren't as lofty. With practice, you'll be able to detect your weak places and increase your performance. ??

2. Be Clear in Your Communication

Always keep your people updated on project objectives, priorities, and critical dates. Effective communication is vital for developing your reputation and winning your team's support, so make sure you give clear instructions and regularly encourage questions and comments.

3. Balance Personal and Professional Life

Building personal ties with your team members is crucial for managing a team. Demonstrate to them that you're capable of a great friendship in addition to your commercial connection. In addition, be the leader that cares about and appreciates the well-being of your staff. If you sense that one of your team members isn't in a good mood, for example, inquire about their day before moving on to work.

4. Apply Constructive Criticism to Your Work

Constructive critique entails expressing good and reasonable perspectives regarding other people's work, including positive and constructive criticism. Constructive criticism is generally offered in a nice rather than hostile style. Give your personnel constructive, thorough, and meaningful feedback while assessing their job. Don't be afraid to praise, but be clear and stern when appropriate.

5. Encourage your Customers to Provide Feedback

Employees are generally hesitant to speak about specific occurrences until prodded. Gather feedback on issues like support, training, and resources, and develop an open-door policy, so your team knows you're happy to listen and help.

After learning how to manage a team effectively, let us get to know a few of the attributes of a team leader.

Chapter 4

Characteristics Of a Team Leader

A competent team leader has numerous features and talents that encourage his colleagues to follow him. Team leaders are born with particular traits, such as compassion and honesty, or formal education and experience enhance leadership talents. The attributes of a good team leader inspire the team's trust and respect and enhance productivity.

Here are a few traits that should be present in a team leader.

1. Communication

A good leader can communicate goals, tasks, and other organizational demands to their team efficiently and straightforwardly. To guarantee that expectations are given to their workers in a way that they can grasp, leaders should be masters of written and verbal communication. Listening closely, speaking, recognizing body language, and being aware of your tone are all part of being a good communicator.

2. Be Productive

Nothing makes you feel better as a team leader than hearing your colleagues eagerly discussing the product or service you generate. The tough component is determining whether it will result in helpful dialog or undesired workplace friction. According to internal communication studies, most mergers and acquisitions do not fail due to conflict. Instead, they fail because of "organizational quiet," caused by a terror of debate. A team leader's responsibility is to inspire proactive talks while keeping them professional and constructive.

3. Be Confident

Have faith in yourself and the choices you're making. Leadership needs moral behavior, consistent performance, open communication, and transparent team transactions. There is no tolerance for doubt or a lack of self-confidence as it will influence your team's morale.

Even if you're thinking outside the box, your bravery and confidence will score you points with the team, enabling you to translate your visionary ideas into reality. A team leader must provide encouragement and guidance to the team while keeping them informed to preserve their self-confidence and perform even better.

4. Ability to Make Decisions

It is unavoidable for a leader to be presented with numerous decisions, so one of the five traits of a strong team leader is making good judgments. Some of the judgments will be minor and personal. Other judgments will be big and profoundly influence the entire team. The capacity to identify the best option distinguishes a strong leader from a bad one. Successful leaders aren't scared to make judgments since they know how to assess the benefits and downsides of numerous alternatives before selecting the ideal one.

5. Self-Awareness

Internal and outward self-awareness are two forms of self-awareness that the finest leaders have. Internal self-awareness allows individuals to comprehend their merits and weaknesses. Their ability to perceive their effect on others and their views termed external self-awareness. Self-awareness allows leaders to see where they need assistance, how they should rely on their team, and where they should strive for progress.

6. Be Respectful

Treat your subordinates, coworkers, and peers with the same respect you desire from others. Your behaviors show your esteem, and if the team sees that you are nice to others, they will follow in your footsteps and treat others with the same respect.

Support and appreciate your team, and you'll notice a difference when each member is prepared to put in a little further effort to achieve your approval. Respect and a pleasant attitude are contagious, and this will aid in developing a helpful and productive work climate.

Now, we shall proceed to know some of the techniques of a team leader.

Strategies of a Team Leader

Every leader in today's competitive business climate establishes organizational goals to realize the organization's vision. One of the many things that a professional leader investigates to attain these goals is the appropriate exploitation of human resources. Client expectations, like company dynamics, are shifting at a rapid pace. To meet clients' high expectations and sustain the business in the market for a long time, the most crucial element is to bring out the finest in the workforce.

The management team and persons in positions of leadership are vital to the overall functioning of a contact center. While communication is the core of great leadership, there are five more vital methods that a contact center manager may utilize to aid a team grow.

1. Rather than Telling, Ask

A contact center manager should consider oneself to be a coach as well. This suggests that instead of continually presenting answers, managers should enable team members the chance to study separately. Of course, it's normal for managers to aspire to share their skills. Still, by asking team members questions and letting the self-discovery process evolve, managers may aid team members learn and better equip them to address challenges on their own in the future. It will also lead to a higher sensation of delight and success.

2. Assemble a Diversified Team

Diverse points of view are helpful. This is crucial to note while recruiting as, as a company owner, you may be hunting for people that think and conduct the same way you do, expecting that this will aid your organization. However, this is challenging to come by, but it also makes no sense in business. A varied team with people from various origins, experiences, and cultures provides an environment to learn from numerous views.

3. Develop Your Coaching and Mentoring Skills

Although being a good coach and mentor is challenging for everyone, it is a critical attribute that a great leader must possess to boost employee performance. It's a time-consuming strategy that needs a lot of effort, but it provides many advantages for excellent team leadership. A great coach must fundamentally encourage, provide feedback, and actively listen to the issues that workers confront.

4. Continue to Learn and Pass on Your Knowledge

Develop your future leaders as well. If necessary, work yourself out of a job and find anything new to do. Teach your team about your faults and equip them with leadership abilities. Some people will be bothered by this, but great leaders will not be; they will be able to let it go.

5. Appreciate Your Peers

When managers fail to appreciate or reward hard effort, workers feel irritated and desire to do less. People could get uninspired and indifferent over time. It may be as easy as expressing "thank you" for a job well done, and offering performance-related incentives is a good approach to proceed.

People want to hear that they are acknowledged constantly and doing a good job. Easy words of encouragement are an easy, economical, and uplifting technique to aid someone if they're doing well.

Now that the strategies of a team leader are clear to you, we will understand how a team ladder stimulates the complete team.

How Can a Team Leader Motivate Their Team?

Motivating your colleagues is undoubtedly at the top of your priorities list as a leader or manager. The motivation levels of your team members may impact their productivity, quality of work, engagement, morale, and interpersonal connections. As a result, it's crucial to build up the appropriate environment for your team's drive to thrive. We'll teach you how in the next part.

1. Pay Your Employees a Fair Wage

When you agree on remuneration for your team, make sure they're equivalent to what other businesses in your field and location are paying. Remember that 26% of engaged workers promise to leave their existing job for a 5% wage rise. So don't let talented folks go because you're paying them too little.

2. Encourage Collaboration

Encourage members to operate as a team by stressing the relevance of collaboration and the link between it and fulfilling group goals. It's important to note that work becomes a lot easier and faster when folks connect. Linking performance to team goals might help drive your team even more.

If collaboration is fostered, individual team members will feel less alone and separated from the workplace. Employees will feel more connected and a part of a wider community, which will encourage them to work harder and enjoy their job.

3. Provide Support

Change often demands the team learning new abilities to notice and comprehend new operating techniques. The team leader must allow the team and individual team members to create and test the new strategy. Ascertain that the necessary degree of development and training has been supplied and that the team and its members have adequate time to verify their newly acquired capabilities.

4. New Ideas Should Be Encouraged

Each team member will feel empowered by carrying out day-to-day chores, offering new ideas, and seeing them through to completion. Give them the opportunity to take initiative, and you'll be impressed at their capacity to come up with amazing ideas.

5. Maintain a Safe Working Environment

Healthy and happy individuals are more engaged and driven, which substantially impacts output, happiness, and creativity. Create an environment where personnel appreciate coming to work and want to spend their time there. Look for settings with a positive attitude, such as wide areas with lots of natural light to add to the cheery feeling. Because most people work from home, having a good work environment includes keeping a healthy and pleasurable online workstation. Ensure that projects and activities are well-organized, that communication is open and transparent, and that everyone is visible, speaking and delivering the same degree of energy as they would physically.

6. Create Possibilities For Growth

When team members develop and expand their abilities, they feel more helpful. Therefore, you should give opportunities for growth and development to your people to motivate and inspire them to generate extraordinary achievements. These adaptations should be directed to the particular needs of each employee and could include:

More training
Setting difficult aspirations
Inviting an employee to watch you
Invest your energy teaching and mentoring someone
Focus on teaching your personnel transferable abilities that they can use for different vocations and encourage them to establish learning goals for themselves.

Motivation is an essential component of any workplace, and you should attempt to keep your personnel engaged and inspired. You'll be assured if you do this.

Chapter 5

Leadership liquid planner

8 Tips for New Team Leaders

There Can Be A Lot On Your Plate As A New Team Leader
Whether you're heading up a new team or taking the reins of an existing one, leading a team for the first time may be terrifying. There's no bedrock of personal experience to rely on. If you're a first-time team leader then you're probably either loving the challenge or thinking a rush for the

door—or a bit of both. Plus, more teams are working remotely and/or are embracing a hybrid style of in-office and at-home work. There is a lot more on the plate for new leaders to tackle today.

1. Make Time To Lead

To be effective, team leaders need to devote time in the role. Too often, this duty is merely added onto someone's already massive work list, so setting the new leader up for failure.

As a team leader, you need to be visible to the team and available to aid them. Part of your new leadership role is to develop a good working environment and community. If you're mostly tied up with your own critical hands-on job, you won't be as visible or able to aid your colleagues. So, be cautious to analyze and re-negotiate your workload before taking on a leadership post in the first place.

2. Get To Know Your Team

Leadership is all about how you influence your team to fulfill its objectives. This is something you'll struggle with if you don't get to know your team members and what makes them tick. While it might be tempting to jump in and start making significant moves from day one, remember that you're not there to exercise your ego.

Take time to listen to your team members; find out what their issues and aspirations are, gather recommendations, and uncover prospective strengths and inadequacies. Only then can you build a leadership plan that has a probability of success. Getting to know who you're working with is the first step to engaging with the team and developing their respect and trust. The ancient adage of listening twice as much as you speak still holds true today.

Touch base with your team, especially those who may be hurting. New team leaders find success holding fast 10-15 minute check-in talks once or twice a week. You may even create calendar slots for "office-hours" where people may arrange appointments and connect with you if they need help or need to chat.

3. Communicate, Communicate, Communicate

Once your team is up and running, it's crucial to keep the communication flowing to develop relationships, monitor progress, and spot dangers and problems. This is particularly effective for managing remote teams since workers could be separated in their tiny work bubbles. When new team leaders communicate consistently and effectively, they often find more engagement from the team. This is because kids see you investing time in them and showing interest in their activities.

Ongoing communication may also boost the types of chats you have with your team. For instance, you have more power to make expectations and duties plain so that everyone knows who's doing what, why and by when. This seems clear but don't assume everyone has your thorough knowledge of the project at hand.

Encourage and embrace innovative ideas. The more your personnel can contribute to the project, the more delighted they'll be. Acknowledge and thank your personnel when they do well and let them know their effort is appreciated. You'll notice that your workers will be more responsive, happier, more productive and empowered to take the initiative on future projects and tasks.

There is a fine balance to how you go about dealing with your personnel. New team managers may easily overcompensate for the distance of remote working or are checking in too frequently, which may raise mistrust that negatively affects the team's productivity. Offer support that is sincere and genuine.

4. Lead By Example

Think about the behaviors you wish and anticipate from your team members. Be cautious to demonstrate such traits yourself. As a team leader, you're the role model, therefore what you say and do will affect the team's work habits and attitudes. That said, it's vital to be yourself and to believe in yourself. If you fake it, you'll rapidly be caught and you'll lose credibility and trust.

Be straightforward, honest and passionate. Treat everyone on the team appropriately, with respect and without preference and you'll find identical behaviors returned. Extend the same respect to the rest of the company as well. Never undermine or criticize other persons or departments in front of the team. Make it evident you're all there to work towards the same aims and successes for the greater picture.

new team leaders communicating at work

5. Reward The Good And Learn From The Bad (And The Ugly)

Recognize good accomplishments and praise them when appropriate. You may not be in a position to give out wage hikes and promotions but a small bit of verbal praise goes a long way in informing your colleagues you are both aware of and glad of their accomplishments.

Be just as swift in addressing unfavorable performance complaints. The longer you leave them, the trickier they'll be to fix. Look for the best in people and understand that blunders will come. When they happen, learn from them and understand how they could be prevented in the future. And whatever you do, don't play the blame game.

If you need to have a harsh chat, do it in private; no public floggings on a conference call, in a meeting, or in a group email. And don't strive to win a popularity contest. Not all your remarks and efforts will be well-received, but if you concentrate more on being everyone's friend instead of being a strong leader, the work will suffer, as will your integrity.

6. Delegate

Trust your workforce to accomplish its job. Being a team leader doesn't suggest you're there to perform other people's work for them or micromanage at each level. Be explicit about what's expected of everyone and let them get on with it. Helping your team members achieve a degree of flexibility helps them to develop their position within your organization on their terms. When difficulties or opportunities come, let the team find a resolution themselves with your support—don't add every new issue to your own to-do list.

Here are some effective delegating tactics for new team leaders to follow.

Establish the desired outcome of a project. Assign responsibility to achieve results rather than a to-do list of tasks. Ask yourself: "What is the result of what we are trying to accomplish?"

Consider who can and should take on the allotted responsibility. Who has the experience to achieve it? Who can do well with this opportunity? Who needs to learn how to execute this task? Who has the time to do it on time?

Define the time specifics. Determine critical milestones, deadlines, and when you expect to have elements of a project accomplished.

Monitor progress and give suggestions. Because you're still responsible for the success or failure of a project and the team; give constructive remarks and coaching as you watch the project's growth.

Ask for ideas and thoughts from the team. Your duty is to determine how things may be improved, who should be involved and how your team may advise on the project's development.

Reflect on the project and get insights regarding what was learned in the process. What did you and the team learn? Identify, convey and document what may be improved. This advice for new leaders is vital to search out better techniques to prosper in future assignments.

7. Be Decisive

When it comes to providing results, don't postpone. Grab the nettle when you need to. It's all too easy to defer important decisions, but ultimately costly for the task at hand and how you're viewed as a leader. If you can't solve a significant challenge, it's helpful to perform a sequence of tiny acts that develop momentum and advance toward the wider target. If things go wrong, take a breath, gather the data you need to make an educated decision and make it.

Don't be terrified of requesting help (it's a sign of strength, not weakness). Consult with your team. Gaining their outside opinion or having the ability to bounce an idea off of them may help you make a more acceptable and meaningful decision. Team management is an ongoing learning process and you will never have all the answers.

To avert difficult decisions down the road, identify the patterns in advance and be prepared to anticipate a solution. Recognizing patterns enables you to make a faster and clearer decision when faced with a similar issue.

8. Enjoy It!

Team leadership is often demanding but usually rewarding. By bringing the correct people and procedures together, you're generating an environment that encourages success and personal growth. Plus, it's a tremendous feeling to be part of a well-oiled team environment that you've positively influenced. So, get out there and just do it!

Whether you see yourself as a future leader or an existing group leader, acquiring the basic team leader talents is critical.

These traits will allow you not simply to become a good leader but will also assist your team function like a well-oiled machine.

So, we recommend you go through this page and obtain an idea of what is important to be a successful team leader:

9 Essential Team Leader Skills Needed To Build A Strong Team

1. Efficient Problem Solving Skills

Having problem-solving talents is integrated in the job description of a team leader. It may be seen as a significant leadership skill.

According to an HBR analysis, problem-solving rated 3rd out of 16 competences that determine a leader's effectiveness.

A good team leader recognizes that difficulties are inevitable and learns to anticipate them. He/She makes sure that the team is well-prepared to tackle any issues and challenges that come their way.

Meanwhile, good leaders don't tend to be overwhelmed by the sheer quantity of difficulties at hand. Instead, they seek to assess the best course of action and establish measures to prevent similar situations from happening in the future.

2. Effective Communication Skills

Leading a team is all about how to properly interact with your people. Whether you are a team leader or the company's CEO, poor communication skills will undoubtedly act as a setback for you.

Having good communication abilities isn't the same as being a great orator. Here are the traits that you may observe in a skilled communicator:

Be clear while communicating. Keep the message precise and understood by your team members. Your workforce should comprehend their aspirations as well as the overall purpose of the firm. Simplicity and clarity are the way to go.

Pay attention to nonverbal communication. Hand gestures, posture, facial expressions, and eye contact will go a long way to get your message across.

Listen more. Prioritize the capacity for everyone to express themselves within a community of people.

Remember to keep a positive mentality.

3. Expert In Delegating Tasks

Efficiently allocating duties is part of the job if you want to be an influential team leader. Good leaders should be able to prioritize the critical tasks and delegate the remaining to the team.

Understandably, many team leaders consider sharing work as purposefully lowering their load.

However, this is so distant from the truth. Assigning tasks to the team enables the team leaders to establish particular targets to the team to reach.

Real delegation is about creating teamwork and assigning accountability to team members. This, in turn, assists the team leader to groom a future leader and prepare their succession.

4. Mediator

Dealing with arguments on a regular basis is part of the team leadership job. Conflicts among team members will impede productivity, weaken the team connection, and establish a hostile culture.

A great leader is also a skillful mediator. When presented with controversy, a good team leader doesn't take sides. He seeks to listen to both sides of the issue and wants to solve the situation.

An excellent strategy to achieve so is by holding sessions with the key players of the conflict and gaining their perspectives about the ongoing circumstance.

Subsequently, instruct them on the significance of collaboration, trust, and transparency.

5. Reward Achievements

Motivation is a critical role in keeping your team's spirit up.

A competent team leader realizes that recognizing people for their efforts is the most effective strategy to improve motivation. Rewarding and appreciating team members substantially enhances not only the team's productivity but also individual performance.

As a team leader, set a common objective of reaching specified milestones.

The end effect of contacting them will be obtaining appreciation for their efforts. This makes sure that the terms are fair. Additionally, make sure that it is not a one-time incident. That is, the recognition should be frequent and prompt.

6. Integrity

The greatest trait for leadership is surely honesty. Without it, no actual success is imaginable, no matter whether it is on a section gang, a football field, in an army, or in an office.
-Dwight D. Eisenhower

Undoubtedly, honesty is one of the fundamental traits of a good leader. Without integrity, no one will see you suitable to lead or trust you. Here's what you can do to encourage honesty in the workplace:

Build a set of strong concepts that'll encompass everything that you do.
Integrate the aforementioned themes in business operations and company culture.

Communicate these guidelines to your personnel and make clear that you don't deviate from them.
Practice what you preach. Don't set rules simply for your personnel to comply. You need to follow them as well.

7. Respects Team Members

To be an excellent team leader, continually give your group of people the respect and trust you want them to provide you with. Working on creating trust and camaraderie with your team involves time, patience, and effort.

Make it a point to inform team members thanks when they perform a wonderful job. Recognize their work publicly.

Proactively ask for feedback and recommendations. Never push your decision on anyone.

Instead, have chats about why you want them to achieve a certain task.

Always give credit where it's due. Never take all the credit for yourself. Always bring teamwork to the forefront.

8. Positive Attitude

Chances are, a hostile team leader will foster a bad team mindset. A fantastic leader has a good attitude about everything they undertake.

Yes, leading a team is no cakewalk in the park. And the difficulties just keep on coming. Having a positive attitude might be the last thing you want to do.

But as a team leader, not only your attitude influences you but also your team. One study found that joyful folks are more effective in various facets of their lives, particularly at work.

A nice work climate will motivate teams to display positive behaviors like creativity, motivation, and camaraderie.

9. Decisive

To be an effective leader, you must be able to make quick and correct decisions. Decision-making is thus a critical part of fundamental team leader qualities.

Most issues won't enable you to appreciate the benefit of brainstorming. Being decisive is to think on your feet and come up with a sensible decision. Being decisive comes with its own perils, and many people seek to wait because of it.

However, don't confuse decisiveness with impulsiveness. Don't be reckless with your decisions. In such instances, consider the viewpoint of the full crew.

Final thoughts on team leadership

So much of our work is done on teams, and that is just going to increase. As organizations attempt to be agile in the face of uncertainty and swift change, the job of the team leader is more vital than ever. In order to lead their teams correctly, leaders must aspire to improve constantly and urge their team members to do the same. As you think about your personal progress, analyze how you execute your various team leader roles and where there is potential for you to become more effective. The greatest leaders continue to grow and change over time.

www.ingramcontent.com/pod-product-compliance
Lightning Source LLC
Chambersburg PA
CBHW070349230526
45471CB00006B/2478